How to Kill Your Giants

~One at a Time~

Volume 2

The Giant of Anxiety

By

Betty L. Wade & Darlene M. Wetzel

ALL WORLDWIDE RIGHTS RESERVED.

All material in this book is protected under International and Federal Copyright Laws and Treaties. All and any parts of this book that are reproduced or transmitted in any form or by any means, electronically or mechanically, including photocopying, recording, or by any information storage and retrieval system should clearly state details of the author / publisher.

Copyright © 2013 Betty L. Wade, Darlene M. Wetzel and KoebelPublishing.Com

1632 Claxton Road, Dawson Springs, KY 42408

Legal Disclaimer: The information in this book is meant to explain God-style freedom and healing from emotional giants. It is not intended to diagnose, advise, treat, replace or judge professional psychiatric and/or medical care. Those matters are best left to qualified physicians. If you find something which you believe should be corrected, please write an email to **Alan@KoebelPublishing.Com**

To see what other Giants we are currently working on and to contact the authors, visit our website: **HowToKillGiants.Com**

Contents

Why We Wrote this Book..5

Why You Should Read this Book......................................5

Authors' Note...6

Note about the Appendix..12

The Giant of Anxiety...13

Chapter 1..13

   Today's Giant from your perspective....................13

Chapter 2..18

   Anxiety Giant faced by a biblical character..........18

Chapter 3..21

   Anxiety Giant from God's perspective..................21

Chapter 4..28

   Anxiety Giant: How Satan attacks.........................28

Chapter 5..31

   Which stone kills the Giant of Anxiety?...............31

Chapter 6..37

   Conversation with God..46

Personal Prayer..48

Obtaining God's Help...48

   Wounded Sheep...50

Anxious Moments...53

Fast Food Devotionals for Anxiety................................57

Appendix...61

- Darlene's Story 61
  - Chapter 1 61
  - Chapter 2 67
- In Recognition 72
  - Darlene wishes to thank 72
  - Betty wishes to thank 73
  - One Last Thing 74
- About The Authors 75

Why We Wrote this Book

Darlene suffered from Depression and was willing to explore and discover its root cause which allowed her to receive help and healing. Today she lives to share her story that others may also enjoy life as it should be. (Please read her story in the Appendix to see what other emotions added to her Depression.)

Betty's husband experienced Depression but was unwilling to deal with its cause. Today she hopes his death will not be in vain, but that this effort will benefit others by offering hope for a brighter future.

Why You Should Read this Book

- ➤ Tired of being a slave to your emotions?
- ➤ Tired of feeling trapped in a cage while others enjoy their freedom?
- ➤ Tired of feeling like a bystander while others enjoy living?
- ➤ Tired of trudging through endless days with no sense of purpose?

That's life when you live with your emotional Giants! Consider the Giant of Anxiety.

Anxiety. It is a part of everyone's life. But when your primary response to every stressor is Anxiety, it's time to make some changes. Follow the authors as they trace the effects of Anxiety back to the roots of fear. Listen to God's repeated instructions to "**be not afraid**." Counter your anxieties with God's word and experience your healing.

Future books in this series will deal with other Giants in your life such as Abandonment, Arrogance, Hopelessness, Fear, Poor Self-Esteem, and Confrontation.

Authors' Note

The tree is cut. The stump remains. Soon new growth is seen on the bark of that stump. The tree may be gone, but life is still there. Life is in its roots. Destroy the roots, and life ceases.

So it is with the problems we face. They enter our lives and plant roots in our very soul. Growth is fueled by our inability to overcome them. Soon they loom over us.

They become our emotional Giants.

These Giants interfere with our lives.

- ➢ They overshadow our view of reality.
- ➢ They rob us of happiness and hope, energy and expectations along with our ability to cope.
- ➢ They stunt our personality, weakening our ability to love ourselves and others as commanded by God (Matthew 22:39).
- ➢ They cloud over our objectivity in viewing these problems with solutions in mind.
- ➢ They dwarf our hopes of ever reaching future goals.
- ➢ They cause emotional cancerous growth in our God-given identity by hiding our view of God.
- ➢ They plant our feet in quicksand with little anticipation of rescue.

Giants can be cut down with medical help, but – like the tree stump – they appear again and again.

Such Giants must be uprooted if they are to disappear permanently.

Giants have been around forever. In biblical times they were real people but posed the same problems as today's emotional Giants.

After leaving Egypt, the Israelites traveled east to the land that God had promised their forefathers. This Promised Land was their inheritance.

They were told to enter and possess it. For some reason they insisted on sending spies for a reconnaissance mission (Deuteronomy 1:22). The result? Real-life giants were discovered.

Fearful, the Israelites rebelled. They wandered in the wilderness for 40 years, and finally – one generation later – entered the land that God had given them.

Guess what? Those same giants that once robbed the Israelites of determination, excitement, hope and a free future were still there – alive and well!

So, how were flesh-and-blood giants destroyed in biblical times? The dramatic account of a young shepherd boy named David tells it all (1 Samuel 17).

The nine-foot giant was called Goliath. For 40 days he intimidated the Israelite king and army with blasphemous words against their God. David determined to put an end to it. Equipped with his faith in God's deliverance, his trusty slingshot and five smooth stones that he had carefully selected from the stream, David faced his opponent.

His weapon was ready, twirled and fired. The stone, guided by God, hit Goliath probably in the only vulnerable place not protected by his military gear. This twelve-fingered, twelve-toed giant fell face-down! Dead!

The problems we face today – like Goliath – need to be met head-on. They are barriers and hindrances that prevent us from experiencing life's best. Their roots are lies and half-truths forming a false belief system. When left alone, they box us in with walls of faulty perception, distorted truth, deformed identity and unfulfilled hopes and dreams.

Fortunately, God equips us with truth, knowledge, understanding and weapons – stones

– to tear down the walls and destroy those roots. Interesting thing about stones and rocks is that they are God-made and plentiful. The weapons for killing our enemies come from God.

What those early giants represented to the Israelite spies, we aren't told. But since human nature doesn't change, we have taken the liberty to name such Giants that we encounter today.

Death of our Giants means renewed life for us. Their destruction involves six areas of strategies.

Chapter 1: Today's Giant from your perspective.

Chapter 2: This Giant as faced by biblical characters.

This eliminates the idea that we are the only ones who have ever experienced this Giant.

Chapter 3: Giant from God's perspective.

Learning God's point of view on situations provides fresh thinking with new insights.

Chapter 4: How Satan, our enemy, attacks us using the Giant.

Knowledge of the enemy's tactics and how

 they are used for our detriment moves us from the defensive zone and provides the hope of defeating the Giant. (Basis for this is found in Judges 7:9-11).

Chapter 5: Which stone kills this Giant?

Account taken from God's word illustrates the perfect **weapon to defeat the enemy**.

Chapter 6: Help in stoning this Giant, using God's names and attributes, God's will, God's word and related readings.

These give added tools in dealing with the enemy's influence and interference. They offer healing for the hurts suffered while under the control of the Giant.

Note about the Appendix:

We included Darlene's story that appeared in Volume 1 Depression. It provides the background for the other Giants that she faced including Anxiety.

Observations:

"Temperamentally anxious people can have a hard time staying motivated, period, because their intense focus on their worries distracts them from their goals."   --Winifred Gallagher

"Never look back unless you are planning to go that way."   --Henry David Thoreau

The Giant of Anxiety

Chapter 1

Today's Giant from your perspective

Anxiety. It has many facets, but unlike diamonds, they aren't pretty. Join a group session as they discuss what this Giant looks like.

Therapist: Today we are going to explore what anxiety is like. Can anyone describe the physical sensations you feel when you are anxious?

Member 1: I feel all jittery like I can't hold still – like I'm pumped full of adrenaline.

Member 2: My heart pounds, and my breathing is fast and shallow.

Member 3: I get an upset stomach. Did I put food in my stomach? Or did I swallow rocks from the cement mixer? I can't tell the difference.

Therapist: Those are good examples. Now let's explore your mental reactions. What goes on in your mind when you're anxious?

Member 1: My brain feels like it's going to burst with thinking that jumps from worry to worry.

Member 2: I remember everything I'm afraid of and get scared all over again.

Member 3: My thinking gets obsessively negative. For example, "I'm never going to get out of this financial mess. Where will my next meal come from? How can I satisfy everyone's demands?"

Therapist: Excellent observations! What about emotionally? How do you feel when you are anxious?

Member 1: For me, I feel uptight – like I'm ready to cry.

Member 2: I get an overpowering sense of dread. I'm sure I've forgotten something critical.

Member 3: I feel flooded with tumbling feelings: scared, worried, frustrated.

Therapist: Can you share how you feel spiritually?

Member 1: I feel very disconnected from God. I forget about the times in the past when He has helped me.

Member 2: Yah, I feel like God is far away when I'm anxious.

Member 3: Sometimes I even get angry with God because I feel so miserable.

Therapist: How does Anxiety impact your life?

Member 1: I get grouchy and irritable. I can't make decisions even about what I should do next. Sometimes I cry. It's very difficult to function at work when I'm anxious.

Member 2: It leaves me unable to function. My energy is zapped, and I can't get going to accomplish anything. I usually end up sitting in front of the TV or computer even though I have things I really need to do.

Member 3: Even when I'm really tired, I can't rest. Forget about sleep. Just put me inside a blender, dump in all the 'what ifs,' turn on the power of doubt and watch everything tumble and churn.

> ➤ Brooding fears garble God's promises.

> ➤ Doubt smashes peace of mind.

> ➤ Pending doom pulls at responsibilities.

What more can I say?!?

Therapist: A professor once told our class a powerful definition for Anxiety – ***a state of disquiet.*** That's certainly what you've described here. Thank you for sharing with us.

* * *

Does any of this sound familiar to you?

Anxiety infiltrates every aspect of our lives. It also displays no prejudice. Regardless of age, social status, accomplishments, educational achievements, gender or vocation, everyone experiences anxious times.

The problem is that some take the professor's definition literally. Anxiety becomes the state where they reside instead of just passing through.

Examples of Anxiety at an extreme in everyday life include: alcoholism or addictions of any kind; abuse to self or others; sexual perversion just to skim the surface.

While brief in their comments, the group members illustrate how disabling Anxiety can be. If your usual response to problems or challenges is getting anxious, then you need to seek God's healing. (There are situations when persistent Anxiety may require medication and counseling concurrently.)

Anxiety is not just a problem today but was present in biblical times as well. Listen as Bathsheba relates her experience with the Giant of Anxiety.

Chapter 2

Anxiety Giant faced by a biblical character

Listen as Bathsheba shares her story (2 Samuel 11).

"My name is Bathsheba. I was the wife of an honorable man, Uriah the Hittite. My husband was away at war fighting for Israel.

"One night a servant knocked at my door. The servant ordered me to come with him to the palace because King David wanted to meet me.

"King David explained that he saw me bathing that evening and thought I was beautiful. One thing led to another, and we slept together.

"He sent me back home with no thought of the consequences of our actions.

"I was alone, knowing I had betrayed Uriah's loyalty and trust. Amidst the whirlwind of thoughts and feelings churning inside me, I experienced morning sickness. I sent word to the King that I was pregnant.

"I was so anxious. How could I tell my husband that I became pregnant while he was away at war? He would know the child was not his because we had not been together.

"What have I done? I have dishonored my husband and brought reproach to the family.

- What will Uriah do to me?

- Will he consider me an adulteress?

- Will he divorce me?

- Will he save my reputation and raise this child as his own?

- Will I be shunned by my neighbors and family?

- Where will I live?

- Will King David protect me?

- Will he have any involvement with this child?

> Will the child be accepted by David's other children?

> Because I disobeyed God's law of fidelity in marriage, will the baby be born healthy?"

* * *

So we understand Anxiety has been a long-term problem affecting many. Read on to see God's point of view.

Observation:

Worry is like a rocking chair. It will give you something to do, but it won't get you anywhere.   --Proverb

Chapter 3

Anxiety Giant from God's perspective

"What an honor it is to interview you, God. May I talk with you about Anxiety?" asked reporter Rob Johnson.

"I'm always willing to talk with my children," answered God.

"God, this feeling of Anxiety, what's it all about?" queried Rob.

"Many people in the world today experience Anxiety, but it's not My will for My children to struggle with it. Let's look at the word, Anxiety, for some clues about feelings associated with it," God replied.

"**A** = Apprehension

"Moses was filled with apprehension when I asked him to lead his people, the Israelites, out of Egypt. Moses begged Me to choose someone who could speak more clearly, but I answered that I would teach Moses how to speak (Exodus 4:10-12).

"Pilot's wife was apprehensive of what would happen to her husband no matter which way he ruled at Jesus' trial. He let the mob's cries to crucify Jesus dictate his action and then washed his hands of Christ's innocent blood (Matthew 27:16-24).

"In Genesis 26:24 I am known as '*Fear Chaser*' (implied). I chase away fears that are outwardly visible and fears hidden deep in the heart," explained God.

"**N** = Nervousness

"I remember," noted Rob, "when the disciples were frightened by a violent storm that came up suddenly on the Sea of Galilee. They were nervous saying, 'How can Jesus sleep through this storm? Doesn't He know we are in danger?' (Matthew 8:23-26)."

"In Psalm 68:35 I am known as the '*God of Empowerment*'. I strengthen My people in their time of need," observed God.

"**I** = Impatient

"The prophet Jeremiah was ridiculed, tormented and thrown in a cistern (Jeremiah 38). In Jeremiah 42 the people that were left in Jerusalem after the Babylonian capture, asked the prophet to pray and ask My direction as to whether they should stay in Jerusalem or flee to Egypt. They promised no matter what I told them, they would obey My instructions.

"However, when Jeremiah gave them My direction to stay in Jerusalem, they became impatient and called him a liar. They refused to obey, fled to Egypt and died there just as I warned them.

"I am *'Slow to Anger'* (Nahum 1:3). I wish people would follow My example.

"Another time people were bringing young children for Jesus to bless (Mark 10:13-16). The disciples grew impatient and tried to push them away. But Jesus told them to allow the little children to come to Him."

"**E** = Expectations

"Zacchaeus (Luke 19:1-10) certainly was flooded with expectations when Jesus stopped in front of the tree, looked up, caught Zacchaeus' eye and commanded him to come down. Then He announced He was going to eat with Zacchaeus that night.

"Can you imagine the thoughts that flashed through his mind?

>*Do I have enough food for a dinner?*

>*Will Jesus criticize or accept me?*

>*Will He insist I give up my lucrative tax collecting job?*

>*Will He make other demands of me?*

>*Will I face rejection from the other Jews?*

"David spent many years being pursued by his enemies. Psalm 13 is an example of David's struggle. He certainly was expecting help when he cried out to Me for relief. I answered him because I am *'Hearer of his Cries'* (Psalm 34:17)," explained God.

"**T** = Tension, Torment

"Satan was sure Job would turn against Me if he tormented him enough (Job 1). Job lost all of his children, possessions and health, but he turned to Me, the one who is *'Quietness Giver,'* (1 Chronicles 22:9) for solace," shared God.

"**Y** = Yearning for Peace

God continued, "One of the criminals who was crucified next to Jesus recognized that He was the King of the Jews and asked for forgiveness (Luke 23:39-43). My Son, Jesus (John 1:34), *'Giver of Peace'* (John 14:27), forgave him and promised him entrance into heaven. It's never too late to ask for the peace I give freely."

"You have spelled the word ANXIETY," Rob noted, "but one letter is missing."

"**X = Unknown** reasons why I am ignored," God responded. "My children become fearful. They fail to bring those concerns to Me. So the feelings escalate and ANXIETY moves in.

"I know this happens. That's why I repeat Myself in My word. Be not afraid. Fear not. Don't be fearful. Sadly, people ignore what I say – either because they are ignorant of My words or because they just don't believe Me."

Rob spoke up, "That's like my car. I had been having a problem, but I ignored it. The situation worsened last week, so I had no choice but to take care of it. I tried to fix it myself, but I finally decided I needed help.

"I took it to a reputable mechanic. He told me the cause – which was something I never considered. He shared what needed to be done to eliminate the problem and the cost of those repairs. I understood that if I didn't do that, my car wouldn't function as it was designed to do," the reporter finished.

"A wise move on your part, Rob. That is exactly what I want people to do when they are suffering from Anxiety. They can't function as I designed them. My plans (Jeremiah 29:11) for them are unfulfilled. I'm the expert. If they come to Me, I know the cause of their problems. I know how to fix it. Unfortunately they would rather believe they can handle things on their own," God concluded.

"**X** has a second meaning – unrevealed. Does that apply?" asked the reporter.

"Yes. It is just as you stated with your car problem. With the help of a computer, the mechanic discovered the true cause. It was something you never considered. Same is true for My children. Things happened to them when they were very young. Those feelings became suppressed, but I know about them," God replied.

"Because You are All-Knowing (Isaiah 46:10 implied)," Rob interjected.

"Precisely. When they are older something unsettling occurs which causes those feelings to surface. When that happens they forget to consult Me first. Instead, they rely on medication which doesn't deal with the true cause of their fears," added God.

"In a nutshell, how would You sum up this situation?" asked Rob.

"Three words. ***'Come to Me.'*** I am here to help them no matter what kind of fears triggers Anxiety for them," concluded God.

* * *

Read on to discover a recipe for Satan's Stew.

Chapter 4

Anxiety Giant: How Satan attacks

Below is Satan's recipe for his favorite stew. The difference between soup and stew is the cooking time and temperature. Stew is cooked at a lower temperature and for a longer period.

Slow simmering blends the ingredients to give a taste that would not be accomplished through a quick boil. This type of cooking constantly applies the heat. Same is true in the emotional realm.

Satan's Anxiety Stew

Base

1. Common Fears
2. Satan's original ingredient*

*Satan's note: My original ingredient – lies and half-truths – is critical for Fear to work at its full potential. Just as human's Vitamin D enables Calcium to work more effectively, so this seasoning allows Fear to work with the following ingredients to produce Anxiety.

Additional Ingredients

As these are available:

1. Stir in unrealistic expectations of self and others

2. Add alarm that separation, being left all alone, provides no human support system

3. Throw in the desire of pleasing others to one's detriment

4. Pour in no control over grief from physically degenerating diseases which could accelerate loss of life

5. Toss in negative words that twist the nature of the heart and soul

6. Mix in lack of acceptance of one's self due to oppressive past experiences

7. Dump in extreme discomfort caused by absence of needed approval from others

8. Add in block of obstruction in experiencing God's love and forgiveness

Simmer for as long as it takes to achieve a continual state of Anxiety.

***

Read on to see how to turn off the heat for this Giant.

Observation:

Worry does not empty tomorrow of its

sorrow. It empties today of its strength.

--Corrie Ten Boom

Chapter 5

Which stone kills the Giant of Anxiety?

The King in Babylon spent his night in the company of the Giant of Anxiety. Only later when he removed the stone to release Daniel did the king discover his Anxiety no longer existed. Listen as he shares this incident (Daniel 6).

"Daniel was a good and disciplined man who worked in the government for me. I am Darius, king of the Medo-Persia Empire.

"Because Daniel distinguished himself, I was making plans to promote him. Unknown to me, this caused jealousy among the other administrators, and they plotted to get rid of him. They brought me a decree stating that anyone who prayed to any god or man beside me for the next 30 days would be thrown into the lions' den. I felt honored by this proposal and signed it into law.

"Daniel was aware of the new law. However, as a devout Jew, he chose to continue his prayers three times a day to God. The group waited under his window.

"As soon as they heard him praying, they quickly reported Daniel for breaking the new law. They reminded me that I was bound to follow the law I had signed.

"I was distraught. But I could find no loophole in my decree. Daniel had to be placed in the lions' den in the evening. I called to him that the God he served would protect him as I sealed the stone over the opening. Once sealed, it assured that no one could rescue him from the lions during the night.

"Returning to the palace, I didn't eat or allow entertainment for the evening. Feeling immobilized by Anxiety, I was wide awake throughout the night.

"At the crack of dawn I ran to the lions' den calling out in hope he was alive. I was relieved when he answered saying God had protected him by closing the mouths of the lions. Immediately I demanded the stone be removed and Daniel lifted out of the den."

King Darius needed the stone removed from the den to rescue Daniel. Removal of the stone wiped out the cause of his Anxiety.

Our anxieties seal in our deepest fears like the stone that sealed in Daniel. We need God to remove the stone of anxious feelings and behaviors to allow access and healing to our long-buried fears. God longs to provide this healing, but will not impose it on us. We have to ask.

Anxiety was not in God's original design for humans. Instead, it is a visible sign of an internal problem. Discovering that root cause is key to accessing God's healing.

Here are some suggestions that can help in your healing process.

- Sit quietly before God.
- Have Bible, journal and pen in hand to note what God reveals.
- Tell God about your Anxiety. Talk just like you would tell your best friend. Share your worries and hurts. If concentration is a problem, enlist the help of a trusted Christian friend, pastor or counselor to pray with you (Matthew 18:20).
- Ask God to bring to mind your earliest memory of feeling anxious.

- Then ask Him to reveal what preceded that Anxiety. (You are seeking the root cause of the Anxiety). You may remember a traumatic experience from childhood that still influences what you have come to believe about yourself and how you face the world.

- Whatever you remember, ask God to enter that memory with His truth and show you the lies you believed that triggered your Anxiety. With the lies exposed, invite God to stone (remove) the Anxiety from your life and replace it with His peace. Also seek God's healing for the hurts you experienced because of believing those lies.

- Claim scriptures about healing such as:

Jeremiah 17:14 – Heal me God and I will be healed; rescue me and I will be rescued for You are my praise.

Psalm 6:2 – Be merciful and heal me, LORD.

- Proceed by asking God to search and bring to mind other times that you felt this way. With each situation you recall, ask God to enter and heal that memory.

After you have prayed about all your memories, remember to thank and praise God for His healing in your life.

When Darlene asked God to reveal the root of her Anxiety, she discovered she didn't feel she was good enough to exist. Now that's an identity issue. She turned to the Bible to see what God thought about her right to live.

> ➢ God created her in His image (Genesis 1:27; Ephesians 2:10).
> ➢ Accepting Jesus, she became a new creation (2 Corinthians 5:17).
> ➢ It is in Jesus that she had the right to exist (John 1:12).

Darlene continued praying, asking God to remove this erroneous belief and replace it with His peace and assurance that, in Him, she is created and has the right to exist.

Internalizing Bible verses and really believing them can be a process. So what are some strategies you can employ if you start to feel anxious? Here are some ideas you can experiment with and build on.

1. Pray, turning your anxious feelings over to God, and thanking Him for the healing He is doing in your life.
2. Play some praise music.
3. Write a long list of things you are grateful for.
4. Remember to laugh. It releases dopamine to calm your body. Watch a comedy show or movie.
5. Exercise. Get out for a walk. View God's creation and draw your attention to Him.
6. Read a book that grabs your interest.
7. Remember to breathe. Inhale thinking, **"Breathe in God's peace,** and exhale thinking **"Breathe out God's love."**
8. Use your imagination to picture Jesus holding the lost lamb – you –, or imagine yourself gathered under the shadow of God's wings as the Psalms talk about (Psalm 17:8; 57:1; 63:7).

The next chapter focuses on God's word and His desires for us.

Chapter 6

Is there help for you?

Absolutely. You have three choices:

1. Ignore this Giant's effects on your life and accept it as "Things-are-what-they-are."

2. Consult with a doctor for relief from your symptoms.

3. Consult with God to get His point of view in this matter.

How to ask God for help is not a mystery. It is very similar to going to a doctor.

Doctor	God
~You experience symptoms that cause you great concern. So you set up an appointment with a doctor.	~You experience symptoms that cause you great concern. So you take it to God (Lamentations 3:57).

Doctor	**God**
~Consulting with him shows your belief that his knowledge and experience will help you.	~Consulting with Him shows your belief that God is Omniscient /All-Knowing (Isaiah 46:10 implied).
~You relate your symptoms to him which signals your belief that he is willing and capable to help you.	~You relate your symptoms which signals your belief that God understands how you feel and is willing and most capable to help you (Psalm 145:9).
~He questions you as to your diet, sleep pattern, exercise and family history. Such information helps him understand possible causes for your symptoms.	~God asks you questions so *you* can understand the basis of your symptoms. Was it caused by actions of others (maybe generational curses), your own actions, your

Doctor	**God**
	faulty perception of incidents due to childhood immaturity?
~You feel confident that he has a good understanding of your health issues.	~You are confident that God has complete knowledge of who you are (Psalm 139:1-4, 13).
~You wait for his evaluation.	~You wait as He reveals what started the Giant (Lamentations 3:26).
~He writes you a prescription.	~God prescribes what you need to do to kill the foundation of this Giant.
~He expects your obedience. You are to follow strictly the	~He expects your obedience concerning what He reveals to you:

Killing The Giant of Anxiety

Doctor | God

Doctor	God
1) frequency and 2) amount of medicine as written.	1) the lies you believed that gave birth to your Giant must be replaced with the healing truth of the situation (Proverbs 12:19; Psalm 51:6; John 8:32)
	2) forgiveness for yourself and/or others* must be given (Luke 6:37).
~Result: control of your discomfort.	~Result: a sad heart which caused a discouraged mood and broke your spirit is changed to a joyful heart, giving you a hopeful future (Proverbs

Doctor	**God**
	15:13; 17:22); your broken-heartedness is healed and your wounds are bound (Psalm 147:3).
	(Physical wounds left unattended fester with infection. They must be cleansed and bandaged to insure healing. The same is true of emotional wounds.
	Such healing releases you of your symptoms. No wounds=no hurts=no more symptoms of your Giant!)
~You receive a bill	~You receive a bill

Doctor	God
requesting monetary payment.	stamped, "Healing paid in full by Jesus."

~This final declaration (bill) is a review of your actions:

~This final declaration (bill) is a review of your actions:

1) you admit that you have a problem that needs addressing;

1) you admit that you have a problem that needs addressing;

2) you meet with a doctor who willingly shares his knowledge with you;

2) you meet with God who willingly declares His love for you (Romans 5:8);

3) you believe the doctor is no respecter of patients. His advice was given not based on your color, education or

3) you believe God is no respecter of persons (Acts 10:34; Romans 10:12, 13; Job 34:19);

Doctor	**God**
economic condition;	
4) you recognize that his know-how is superior to your knowledge;	4) you recognize that God is absolute, final authority (Isaiah 43:13 implied);
5) you listen as possible causes for your symptoms are given;	5) you listen as God reveals that everyone is born with a sin nature. Sins/wrong doings separate you from God (Romans 3:23) resulting in the existence of Giants;
6) you are told that medicine is available;	6) you are told that Jesus, God's only begotten Son, died and three days later rose from the grave. He did this so you could enjoy a personal relationship

Doctor	**God**
	with God as your heavenly Father (1 Corinthians 15:3; Galatians 1:4; Revelation 1:5-6)
7) possible medications are discussed along with their side effects;	7) as your transgressions are revealed, necessary action is expected. Sin requires confession and forgiveness (1 John 1:9; Romans 10:9, 10; Acts 3:19) taking note that belief in Jesus' death and resurrection makes this all possible (John 1:12; 1 John 4:10);
8) you accept his prescription;	8) you accept what God's word says. You meet His requirements concerning the sin issue and then enjoy a new status – child of God

Doctor	**God**
	(Romans 8:16; Galatians 3:26);
9) you fill the prescription and wait in expectation for it to work on your symptoms;	9) as you discover the root cause of your Giant, you wait for God's revelation for killing the Giant. Just as important, you ask God for His healing from the hurts caused by the Giant;*
10) if the medicine works, you enjoy life pain-free when symptoms are physically based.	10) with complete obedience to God, you are filled with joy, peace and hope (Romans 15:13). Permanent relief.

Conversation with God

God's Love: God, I believe You love me (1 John 4:19). I believe You desire to have a close, personal relationship with me (Psalm 91:14-16; Hebrews 13:5).

Sin: Like everyone else, I was born with a nature – called sin (wrong doings) – that separates me from You (Romans 3:10, 23). Sin robs me of life with You, and only life – found in blood – can restore what was stolen from me (Romans 6:23).

Jesus' Life and Death: So You sent Your only begotten Son, Jesus, to offer His life – His blood – as payment for my sins (Isaiah 53:12; John 3:16; Romans 5:8). I accept Jesus' death on my behalf. Because of His death, penalty for my sins was paid (Proverbs 16:6; Acts 10:43; 1 Peter 1:18, 19). I believe that Jesus died but also was raised from the dead and lives today with You in heaven, ever presenting my needs to You (Romans 6:4; 8:11, 34).

Confession: I therefore confess that I am a sinner by birth (Romans 5:12). I believe that Jesus is Lord who paid my sin-penalty with His own death (1 Corinthians 15:3; 1 John 2: 1, 2).

I believe that You, God, raised Jesus from the grave (1 Peter 1:21; Acts 13:34; 1 Corinthians 15:4). What I believe, I accept as truth. I ask for forgiveness of my sins through the blood of Jesus shed for me (Daniel 9:8, 9; Acts 3:19).

God's Word: Your Word – the Bible – says that I am now saved. It is only by Your grace and mercy that this is possible. It is not based on what I do. Salvation can't be earned by my own doings (Isaiah 64:6; Romans 10:9, 10; Ephesians 2:8, 9).

New Creation: Because of this confession, I am now a new person (Romans 6:6, 14; 2 Corinthians 5:17; Galatians 5:16-26; Ephesians 4:22-24; Colossians 3:9). As a new creation, I live a life pleasing to You, my heavenly Father (2 Corinthians 5:20; Ephesians 4:25, 31, 32*; Colossians 3:2, 12).

Healing Accepted: I also understand that forgiveness of sins allows me to accept Your healing for the hurts that sins – mine and others – have caused (2 Chronicles 7:14).

Personal Prayer

Heavenly Father,

It's so frustrating to be knotted-up with anxieties and fears. I pray for Your touch of healing for relief. I do want to breathe in Your peace and breathe out Your love. Thank you for giving me Your truth. Thank you for showing the root cause for my feelings. Thank you for the freedom You bring into my life. Thank you for caring about me.

Amen.

*Read more about this subject in

Forgiveness God Style by Betty L. Wade

Obtaining God's Help

through God's Names and Attributes:

~Anchor for the soul – Hebrews 6:19

~Arms everlasting – Deuteronomy 33:27

~Balm of Gilead – Jeremiah 8:22

~Heals the brokenhearted – Psalm 147:3

~God of all comfort – 2 Corinthians 1:3

~God of hope – Psalm 71:5

~Lifter of those bowed down – Psalm 146:8

~L ORD who heals you – Exodus 15:26

~Restorer of my joy – Psalm 51:12

~Shelter from the storm – Isaiah 25:4

~Shepherd – Psalm 23:1

~Wiper of tears – Isaiah 25:8

through God's Will:

~to have a positive attitude – 1 Thessalonians 5:16-18

~to have peace – 2 Thessalonians 3:16

~to not fear – Lamentations 3:57

~to give Him our cares – Psalm 55:22

through God's Word:

~binds up the brokenhearted and sets prisoners free – Isaiah 61:1

~give God all your cares and concerns – 1 Peter 5:7

~anxiety is a heavy weight – Proverbs 12:25

~be anxious for nothing – Philippians 4:6

~banish anxiety from your heart – Ecclesiastes 11:10

~do not worry about defending yourself – Luke 12:11

~being anxious accomplishes nothing – Luke 12:25

through related readings:

Wounded Sheep

I was following my shepherd, minding my own business, when I noticed something of interest in the mountains. I started climbing, easily taking the turns of the path. When I looked behind me, I was startled to see that the shepherd and flock were not there.

Night was falling, and I was petrified. I could "smell" the dangers around me just like the predators could probably "smell" my fear.

I tried to find my way out, but in the darkness I stumbled. I stepped off the path and ended up in the briers. My legs stung. I wanted to cry out, but that would surely signal my presence where I did not belong. I was totally alone!

My fear intensified when I saw movement coming toward me. This is my end, I thought.

Then I heard my shepherd's voice. He had found me. All strength left my body. With gentle hands and strong arms he lifted me to his shoulders. He wrapped my limp body around his warm neck. I was safe, and fear left.

All the way home my shepherd, my savior, spoke softly to me. He told me how he missed me. He cared so much for <u>me</u> that, taking no thought of his weariness after a long day's work, he started his search, determined not to return home empty-handed.

As he quietly sang songs of thanksgiving over me, I closed my tired eyes. What made <u>me</u> so special? I realized it wasn't me at all. It was the shepherd's <u>love</u> for me that sent him on this rescue mission.

The burning of my legs couldn't keep sleep away. I knew that healing was already taking place. I knew that when my shepherd put me down, I would be back in the fold where I belonged. I might be a sheep by age, but inside I am a vulnerable lamb.

A lam**b** with **b**urdens, **b**ungling ways and **b**lemishes, **b**ound to go my own way. But my Savior turned those "**B**'s" upside down. He was my lam**p** that led me back home. Never again would I desire to stray from his side.

Today, prayer warriors lift this sheep when all strength is gone. They are the burden-bearers when I am engulfed by the mountain of blackness, uncertain of where I am going. They resemble the Good Shepherd, carrying me to where I belong.

Observation:

God's clock is always on time.

--Adele Saffady

Anxious Moments

Walk with Moses as he trudges up the hill followed by Aaron and Hur (Exodus 17:8-13). Listen as he talks to the LORD.

LORD, you know we didn't pick this battle. The Amalekites have been following us – attacking Your people and plundering them (Deuteronomy 25:17, 18).

You know these people have not experienced freedom too many days. They are not warriors. Just the opposite. To confront their slave masters resulted in physical abuse. These, Your children, have been conditioned to not resist.

Now some men find themselves in Joshua's troop to fight these marauders. A novice commander and inexperienced soldiers. Grounds for Anxiety.

I am anxious for them and the outcome of this first encounter with our enemy. And they are most anxious because of what is expected of them. To fight. To win.

LORD, they saw Your mighty hand in delivering them from Egypt's bondage. They experienced Your protection while crossing the Red Sea. With their own eyes they witnessed the waters close upon Pharaoh's army, sending dead bodies to the shore.

Now I ask You to show them victory in this battle. May their Anxiety be relieved as they see me holding up my hands with Your staff to heaven, calling down Your mercy and favor on this, Your people.

Teach them that the battle is Yours. They don't enter the fighting arena in their own strength or expectations. Just as You provided an ample supply of water from an unlikely source – a rock – so may they understand that their ability to confront the enemy and win this battle also comes from You.

The three men stand on the hilltop in plain view of Joshua and his chosen fighters. As long as Moses has the physical strength to keep his arms raised, the Israelites have the advantage over the Amalekites.

But tired arms need resting. When lowered, the Amalekites advance. The war is then fought on two fronts:

~**external**, suffering from the enemy's weapons;

~**internal**, experiencing the pain of worry, fear, uneasiness and threats.

No support from the Lord means no victory for His people. Fortunately Aaron and Hur operate in the Lord's wisdom. They select a nearby rock on which Moses sits. His arms are now on a level for them to easily support with their own hands.

~This rock provides the soldiers with the emotional support for the all-day encounter.

~This rock provides the physical support that allows Moses, Aaron and Hur to intercede on behalf of the Lord's people.

~This rock is the support when Apprehension says, "There is nothing solid on which to depend."

~This rock is the support when anticipation of impending doom whispers, "There is no hope. All is lost."

~This rock is the support when Distress shouts, "You can't handle this situation!"

~This rock provides physical rest and emotional security.

~This rock refocuses attention. Victory is the LORD's to give, not ours to win. Self-dependence and doubt, uncertainty and lack of confidence are stoned when we lift our eyes to the LORD, our **Rock of Strength** (Psalm 62:7 implied).

Observation:

Someone once said, "Hope springs eternal." One situation changes, one phase of life ends, one season closes. These are but the beginning of something new. Life means change. Change is not something to dread or hate. It is the make-up of living. Looking at change through the eyes of hope gives a peek into the future, for each change becomes a knot in the cord of life to help move us forward into another phase." Youth's Journey

Fast Food Devotionals for Anxiety

May I recognize today the opportunities to enjoy **Abundant Life** (John 10:10) so that Your plans for me will be accomplished.

God, Your name is **Anchor** (Hebrews 6:19). Keep me steady during rough times and through storms of uncertainty.

When I am weary and weak, I feel Your support from **Arms Everlasting** (Deuteronomy 33:27) underneath me.

You are **Author and Finisher of Our Faith** (Hebrews 12:2). There is no lack in You or for those who trust and worship You.

You are **Beneficent** (Psalm 119:68 implied). May I not take for granted the blessings of Your love and protection from ill winds and uncomfortable situations.

When my plans take a different direction, I remember that You are **Change Maker** (Daniel 2:21). I watch to see how You reveal deep and hidden things.

Out of ruin, You make my wilderness of bad decisions like Eden and my desert of painful consequences like Your Garden. In You I find gladness and joy, thanksgiving and music (Isaiah 51:3). You are my **Comforter** (Isaiah 51:12).

In the midst of baffling circumstances, I understand what is to be accomplished because You show me Your point of view. You are **Commander of Adversities** (Psalm 107:25-30 implied).

Sometimes my life's path comes to a dead-end. I cannot see beyond the bend, but I have no fear. The redirection of my feet passes through You, for You are my **Cornerstone** (1 Peter 2:6).

Moses stood before the burning bush and heard Your voice. So, as I face burning issues, help me hear Your directions for You are **Dweller in the Bush** (Deuteronomy 33:16).

Be my **Encircling Shield** (Psalm 91:4 implied). Put my soul and spirit in a safe place so Your beauty may be reflected today.

When fear invades my mind and dread encompasses my emotions, let me remember that I am not alone for You, my God, are my **Ever-Present Help** (Psalm 46:1).

You dressed the fish of the deepest waters with beautiful colors long before we ever saw them. You created and named stars long before telescopes discovered them. I rest easy in the thought that You know everything about my life – beginning to end. You **Ensure Your Servant's Well-Being** (Psalm 119:122).

Today, I refuse to be troubled in my spirit or allow anything or anyone to rob me of my peace of mind and joy in You, my Lord. You are my **Giver of Peace** (John 14:27).

You are **Giver of Quietness** (1 Chronicles 22:9). May I have a calm spirit that allows me to listen for and follow Your voice throughout today's activities that such experiences might be full and pleasant.

I rest in the thought that You are **God Who Holds in His Hand All (My) Ways** (Daniel 5:23).

When my plans don't work out as I had hoped, I will not be distressed. Like Noah and the ark, sometimes for my safety You intervene. You are **Lord Who Shuts the Door** (Genesis 7:16).

You said that many are the afflictions of the righteous; but You deliver him out of them all (Psalm 34:19). You are **Merciful** (Genesis 19:16), my shock-absorber for sorrow and affliction.

You are God, my **Strength** (Exodus 15:13). Wrap me in Your arms when life's demands are too great.

I will not be anxious over meeting deadlines, living up to others' expectations or pressures imposed on me for I remember that You are my **Sustainer** (Psalm 3:5).

Appendix

Darlene's Story

Chapter 1

Have you heard of big "D" and little "d"? Little "d" is depression that everyone experiences at times in their lives. For example missing an important event due to illness, getting into a fender bender with your new car or having a big fight with your spouse. Big "D" is Depression at a mental illness level. Mental illnesses are disorders of the brain that disrupt a person's thinking, feeling, mood and ability to relate to others.

Mental illnesses can affect persons of any age, race, religion or income. These are more common than cancer, diabetes or heart disease. There will be 25 million Americans who will have an episode of major Depression this year alone.

The good news is that treatment helps. As a diabetic takes insulin, most people with serious mental illness need medication. But as a rule, medication controls only the symptoms and is not in itself a cure. Treatment often includes counseling and lifestyle changes. Some people recover with this support. Others face a difficult battle.

In 1998 I became severely Depressed. I had been depressed at other times in my life, but nothing as disabling as this. I thought I had let everyone down, was a failure and didn't deserve to live. (*Giant of Abandonment*)

These depressive thoughts birthed years of struggle and despair as I pushed myself to reach the unattainable goals of trying to feel better and pleasing other people. When I failed and someone was angry with me, I would feel anxious and even suicidal, with anguish and hopelessness. (*Giant of Anxiety*)

I was unable to keep my position as a social worker. Immobilized, this left me unable to keep up with daily household tasks like cooking and laundry. I felt useless. (*Giant of Hopelessness*)

My years of Depression and repeated hospitalizations took a terrible toll on my family. My husband felt the doctors were over-medicating me and urged me to stop taking my medicine. (*Giant of Arrogance*) He hated that I was so sedated and barely functioning. I hated the rapid weight gain, the blinding migraines and feeling dazed all the time.

When I would listen to him, and stop taking my medication, it would create another crisis in my treatment and usually require another hospital stay. I didn't know who to listen to. (*Giant of Unanswered Questions*) I was in an encompassing turmoil. (*Giant of Anxiety*) I wanted to please my husband, but I felt terrible when I went off my meds. (*Giant of Confrontation*)

Eventually my treatment team convinced me that I really did need the medications. I decided that taking the medicine with all the life-changing side effects was better than being in the hospital. But the doctors couldn't find a med that would ease my Depression without triggering the migraines. (*Giant of Waiting*)

We tried many different medications. Finally they found a combination that would lighten my mood so I could function at a minimal level. Still I remained under intensive medical and psychological treatment.

The strain on my husband was overwhelming. A two-time kidney transplant survivor with medical issues of his own, he was exhausted. Trying to take care of me, pulling the load of parenting, keeping up with the housework and working full time was an incredibly difficult ordeal.

When my husband lost his job in 2002 things got even worse. Financially we were ruined. We filed for bankruptcy and struggled to keep our home. Once again I felt like a failure. (*Giant of Broken Promises*)

He became even angrier at my illness, the doctors and just the whole situation. He would argue with everything the doctors said, criticize me (Giant of Negative Words) for not getting any housework done, and complain when dinner wasn't on the table at his arrival home. (*Giant of Anger*)

I would crumple in despair which fueled suicidal thoughts. I couldn't bear his disapproval and lack of recognition that I was struggling so hard to hang on. (*Giant of Despair*)

My children were 10 and 13 when Depression hit. I taught them about my mental illness and supported them the best I could but still felt like a failure as a mother. My mother-in-law would drop everything and take care of the children and house during my hospitalizations.

My daughter was so afraid that I would be gone when she woke up that she refused to sleep in her room. (*Giant of Anxiety*) She would only go to bed in my room. Eventually we got her in counseling. After seven months we were able to gradually move her back to sleeping by herself.

My son, age 13, was busy with his friends and youth group activities. His goal was to stay out of the house as much as possible. As he got older he became closer to me.

With my husband's refusal to take me to the hospital my son was pushed into the role of caregiver. (*Giant of Abandonment*) When he got his driver's license, he would take me to the hospital to be evaluated for admission and pick me up after discharge. (*Giant of Responsibility*) He seemed to handle my illness pretty well.

Throughout the Depression I was plagued by

hearing voices. This is a symptom of Depression which occurs sometimes. The voices would ridicule me and tell me that I didn't deserve to live. (*Giant of Negative Words*) The thought of ending my life was a frequent companion that I struggled against.

My mother was deceased. My father had remarried and moved to Florida. (*Giant of Grief*) He tried to be supportive both emotionally and financially, but he thought depression was caused by sin. Two more tentacles of failure squeezed me—that of a daughter and of a Christian. Two more failures—my father and, in my mind, my Heavenly Father's. (*Giant of Abandonment*)

My extended family and Bible study women were very helpful. They called, sent cards, brought meals and, most of all, prayed.

Chapter 2

My spiritual journey was marked by ebbs and flows. When I first became Depressed my faith stayed strong. I attended church when I could muster the energy, and my minister and church family were supportive.

It was a very small congregation, and they needed everyone to carry multiple responsibilities. I played the piano for church, headed up the Bishop's Committee and other tasks as they requested. Needless to say, I couldn't keep up with all this activity. (*Giant of Busyness*)

Eventually I transferred membership to a larger church that had a youth program for the kids to participate in. I believe God was at work in this move because of the spiritual growth I saw in my children.

However, I felt terribly guilty for leaving the smaller church. (*Giant of Guilt*) When I could get myself to church, I cried through the service and struggled in my relationship with God. (*Giant of Grief*)

After nearly 25 years of a poor marriage and the stress of my illness, we divorced. (*Giant of Failure*) We were broken individuals. Once the house sold we were able to part. I moved into an apartment on my own for the first time in my life. There was such relief from the fighting and verbal abuse. I was able to gain a little equilibrium. I was still, however, hospitalized once or twice a year.

I avoided some hospitalizations by attending a Partial Hospitalization program. This is an intensive day treatment program which includes both individual and group therapy. There are also classes that range from nutrition and sleep routine to anger management. It is used as both a step-down program after a hospital stay and an intervention to contain a major Depressive episode before hospitalization is necessary.

While I was somewhat better, more stressors piled in: my therapist died suddenly, my father died and my ex-husband died. (*Giant of Abandonment*) My medical team, my therapy group cohorts and my group of friends supported me as I struggled to keep my balance.

A friend invited me to experience God's grace

and healing. After 14 years of Depression and many prayers asking for God's healing, I wasn't expecting much. But I agreed to pray with her because I hoped for relief.

First we asked God to break the generational curse of depression. I could trace Depression back at least three generations. Next I asked forgiveness for believing Satan's lies that I was a failure and didn't deserve to exist. Believing these lies blocked my relationship with God (*Giant of Lies*) but was restored when God brought His truth into my memory.

Then we talked and prayed for hours. With the Holy Spirit's guidance we returned to my first memory of feeling like a failure. We asked Jesus to enter this memory and heal the hurt. We prayed for each memory God brought to my mind. God healed those memories so that I can think about the experiences without feeling emotional pain.

God showed me that I have the right to be alive in Him-that He saved me not because of my doing but because of His mercy (Ephesians 2:8). I immediately felt a great weight lift off my shoulders! I was filled with deep joy that I had not experienced in many years.

However, I knew from reading the Bible (Ephesians 6:11-13) that Satan would not give up easily. So I needed to prepare for an onslaught of attacks that would rob me of my new-found joy. After all, the Giant of Depression did not come from God. It came from God's enemy, Satan. Satan can't attack God directly, so he attacks God's creation, us.

He did try to enter my mind with doubts and fears about the healing God was doing. I felt like I was in combat. (*Giant of Spiritual Warfare*) Each time these negative thoughts came to mind, I would recognize they were coming from the enemy. (*Giant of Negative Words*) I prayed to rebuke them in the name of Jesus and commanded them to leave.

To assist me in the battle of Satan's attacks, I pray each day and put on the complete armor of God which Paul wrote about in Ephesians 6:14-17. I do this every morning when I first get up. I also studied my identity in Christ Jesus. The Bible said I am made in the image of God (Genesis 1:26), a new creation in Christ (2 Corinthians 5:17), and that Christ lives in me (Galatians 2:20; Romans 8:10). Recognizing these truths is helping me let go of the idea and feeling that I am a failure. (*Giant of Failure*)

While years of counseling and medication had laid the groundwork, they had not made me well. God did. The Depression vanished! I still have some struggles and a lot to learn, but God is working in my life, healing painful memories, changing behavior patterns and establishing a joy that permeates my whole being.

In Recognition

Darlene wishes to thank...

...our team, Jan, Carolyn and Al, who offered their time and talent to pray, read, edit and publish these Giants.

...friends and family who supported me through the difficult path of Depression including my children, Amy and Luke, Aunt Ernestine, my church, friend Judy and all in the Walk 'n Talk group.

...my treatment team for the wonderful care I've received over the past years. Also, my Wednesday night cohorts and our therapists Craig and John.

...my friend, Betty, who invited me on this journey and nurtured me each step of the way.

...and glorify God who by working in us is able to do more than we can ask or even imagine (Ephesians 3:20, 21). This book is a testament to God's awesome power.

Betty wishes to thank...

...cousin Jan and sister Carolyn for their endless reading, editing and rereading this material. Your hours of selfless labor are most appreciated.

...brother-in-law Al for countless hours of study and work in order to publish this series. Couldn't do this without you.

...friend Darlene for having the teachable spirit needed to experience miraculous healing and obey God's directive to share her story with others.

...most of all her heavenly Father. Thank you for all the tough times that you brought into my life, and the Giants that You stoned so I could be the person I am today. May our readers also experience Your deliverance. May they see You as *God Who Holds in His Hand (Their) Life and All (Their) Ways* (Daniel 5:23).

One Last Thing...

Thank you so much for reading our book. If you enjoyed this book or found it useful, we would be very grateful if you'd post a short review on Amazon. Your support really does make a difference. We read all the reviews personally which enables us to get your feedback and helps us make our books even better.

Thanks again for your support! We look forward to hearing from you. At this time we haven't learned to use Twitter and Facebook but hope to learn how in the near future. You can contact either of us at our website: **HowToKillGiants.Com**

Our other books on Amazon:

How to Kill Your Giants ~ One at a Time ~ Vol. 1 The Giant of Depression

Forgiveness ~ God Style ~ A Biblical Guide To Totally Forgive by Betty L. Wade

About The Authors

Darlene M. Wetzel was born and raised near Lansing, Michigan. She has two grown children. She earned her Bachelor's degree in psychology from Spring Arbor University and later earned her Masters of Social Work at Michigan State University. She pursued her dream of helping people by working at the American Cancer Society, Hospice and the University of Michigan's Mott Children's Hospital. In 1998 she experienced the onset of Major Depression. She struggled with the illness for 14 years before God graciously healed her on September 11, 2012. She felt led to tell her story in hopes that it may help others.

Betty L. Wade was born and raised in the Detroit, Michigan area. She graduated from Michigan State with a degree in Elementary Education. The next 32 years were spent teaching in public schools. She started teaching Sunday school at the age of 14, and has held various church jobs - Sunday school Superintendent, Christian Education Director and Praise and Worship pianist. She is passionate about her love for God, studying His word, writing and helping others.

Notes:

Notes:

Notes:

Notes:

Made in the USA
Charleston, SC
14 January 2014